# ADDRESSES

*Images by*

# ANNE GEDDES

ANNE GEDDES ™

ISBN 1-55912-346-X

© Anne Geddes 1994

Published in 1996 by Cedco Publishing Company,
2955 Kerner Blvd, San Rafael, CA 94901.
First USA edition 1996.
Second printing, February 1997

Produced by Kel Geddes
Color separations and design by MH Group
Artwork by Bazz 'n' Else
Printed through Colorcraft, Hong Kong

Please write to us for a FREE FULL COLOR catalog of our fine Anne Geddes
calendars and books, Cedco Publishing Company, 2955 Kerner Blvd.,
San Rafael, CA 94901.

# ANNE GEDDES

$A$nne Geddes, an Australian-born photographer, resident in Auckland, New Zealand, has won the hearts of people internationally with her unique and special images of children.

Not only is her work widely recognized and sought after in the commercial field, but her exceptional images have received resounding critical acclaim, attracting a host of professional awards.

Many of Anne's distinctive and memorable photographs have been published internationally, including the prestigious USA's *"Life"* Magazine, Germany's *"Tempo"*, the *"London Sunday Mirror"* and The News of the World *"Sunday Magazine"* to name but a few.

Anne's work mirrors the joy and love found in the children who will form the future of the planet. After all, she says, *"To be able to capture on film the innocence, trust and happiness that is inherent in the next generation is a very special responsibility. It's work that rewards me daily with a great deal of personal satisfaction."*

Another major challenge in Anne's life is to ensure that the photography of children is widely accepted as an art form that legitimately competes with any other form of photographic speciality.

Anne is married to her friend and business partner Kel. Together they have two children.

**A**

Name _____

Address _____

_____

Phone _____


Name _____

Address _____

_____

Phone _____


Name _____

Address _____

_____

Phone _____


Name _____

Address _____

_____

Phone _____

## A

Name _____

Address _____

_____

Phone _____


Name _____

Address _____

_____

Phone _____


Name _____

Address _____

_____

Phone _____


Name _____

Address _____

_____

Phone _____

A

Name

Address

Phone

Name

Address

Phone

Name

Address

Phone

Name

Address

Phone

# B

Name _____

Address _____

Phone _____

Name _____

Address _____

Phone _____

Name _____

Address _____

Phone _____

Name _____

Address _____

Phone _____

# B

Name _____

Address _____

_____

Phone _____


Name _____

Address _____

_____

Phone _____


Name _____

Address _____

_____

Phone _____


Name _____

Address _____

_____

Phone _____

**C**

Name

Address

Phone

Name

Address

Phone

Name

Address

Phone

Name

Address

Phone

# C

Name

Address

Phone

Name

Address

Phone

Name

Address

Phone

Name

Address

Phone

# C

Name _____

Address _____

_____

Phone _____


Name _____

Address _____

_____

Phone _____


Name _____

Address _____

_____

Phone _____


Name _____

Address _____

_____

Phone _____

# D

Name

Address

Phone

Name

Address

Phone

Name

Address

Phone

Name

Address

Phone

# D

Name

Address

Phone


Name

Address

Phone


Name

Address

Phone


Name

Address

Phone

D

Name

Address

Phone

Name

Address

Phone

Name

Address

Phone

Name

Address

Phone

# E

Name _____

Address _____

_____

Phone _____


Name _____

Address _____

_____

Phone _____


Name _____

Address _____

_____

Phone _____


Name _____

Address _____

_____

Phone _____

# E

Name

Address

Phone


Name

Address

Phone


Name

Address

Phone


Name

Address

Phone

# E

Name

Address

Phone


Name

Address

Phone


Name

Address

Phone


Name

Address

Phone

# F

Name

Address

Phone

Name

Address

Phone

Name

Address

Phone

Name

Address

Phone

# F

Name

Address

Phone

Name

Address

Phone

Name

Address

Phone

Name

Address

Phone

## F

Name

Address

Phone


Name

Address

Phone


Name

Address

Phone


Name

Address

Phone

# G

Name

Address

Phone


Name

Address

Phone


Name

Address

Phone


Name

Address

Phone

# G

Name

Address

Phone


Name

Address

Phone


Name

Address

Phone


Name

Address

Phone

# G

Name

Address

Phone


Name

Address

Phone


Name

Address

Phone


Name

Address

Phone

# H

Name _____

Address _____

_____

Phone _____


Name _____

Address _____

_____

Phone _____


Name _____

Address _____

_____

Phone _____


Name _____

Address _____

_____

Phone _____

# H

Name

Address

Phone

Name

Address

Phone

Name

Address

Phone

Name

Address

Phone

**H**

Name

Address

Phone

Name

Address

Phone

Name

Address

Phone

Name

Address

Phone

I

# I

Name

Address

Phone

Name

Address

Phone

Name

Address

Phone

Name

Address

Phone

# J

Name _____

Address _____

_____

Phone _____


Name _____

Address _____

_____

Phone _____


Name _____

Address _____

_____

Phone _____


Name _____

Address _____

_____

Phone _____

J

Name _____

Address _____

_____

Phone _____


Name _____

Address _____

_____

Phone _____


Name _____

Address _____

_____

Phone _____


Name _____

Address _____

_____

Phone _____

## J

Name

Address

Phone


Name

Address

Phone


Name

Address

Phone


Name

Address

Phone

K

Name

Address

Phone

Name

Address

Phone

Name

Address

Phone

Name

Address

Phone

Name

Address

Phone

Name

Address

Phone

Name

Address

Phone

Name

Address

Phone

K

Name_____

Address_____

_____

Phone_____


Name_____

Address_____

_____

Phone_____


Name_____

Address_____

_____

Phone_____


Name_____

Address_____

_____

Phone_____

# L

Name _____

Address _____

_____

Phone _____


Name _____

Address _____

_____

Phone _____


Name _____

Address _____

_____

Phone _____


Name _____

Address _____

_____

Phone _____

L

Name _____ _____

Address _____

_____

Phone _____


Name _____

Address _____

_____

Phone _____


Name _____

Address _____

_____

Phone _____


Name _____

Address _____

_____

Phone _____

# L

Name

Address

Phone

Name

Address

Phone

Name

Address

Phone

Name

Address

Phone

M

Name

Address

Phone

Name

Address

Phone

Name

Address

Phone

Name

Address

Phone

# M

Name

Address

Phone

Name

Address

Phone

Name

Address

Phone

Name

Address

Phone

Name _____

Address _____

_____

Phone _____


Name _____

Address _____

_____

Phone _____


Name _____

Address _____

_____

Phone _____


Name _____

Address _____

_____

Phone _____

# N

Name _____

Address _____

_____

Phone _____


Name _____

Address _____

_____

Phone _____


Name _____

Address _____

_____

Phone _____


Name _____

Address _____

_____

Phone _____

Name

Address

Phone

Name

Address

Phone

Name

Address

Phone

Name

Address

Phone

Oh no!

Name _____

Address _____

_____

Phone _____


Name _____

Address _____

_____

Phone _____


Name _____

Address _____

_____

Phone _____


Name _____

Address _____

_____

Phone _____

# P

Name _____

Address _____

_____

Phone _____


Name _____

Address _____

_____

Phone _____


Name _____

Address _____

_____

Phone _____


Name _____

Address _____

_____

Phone _____

# P

Name

Address

Phone

Name

Address

Phone

Name

Address

Phone

Name

Address

Phone

# P

Name

Address

Phone


Name

Address

Phone


Name

Address

Phone


Name

Address

Phone

Name

Address

Phone

Name

Address

Phone

Name

Address

Phone

Name

Address

Phone

R

Name_____

Address_____

_____

Phone_____


Name_____

Address_____

_____

Phone_____


Name_____

Address_____

_____

Phone_____


Name_____

Address_____

_____

Phone_____

R

Name _____

Address _____

_____

Phone _____


Name _____

Address _____

_____

Phone _____


Name _____

Address _____

_____

Phone _____


Name _____

Address _____

_____

Phone _____

# R

Name

Address

Phone

Name

Address

Phone

Name

Address

Phone

Name

Address

Phone

# S

Name_____

Address_____

_____

Phone_____


Name_____

Address_____

_____

Phone_____


Name_____

Address_____

_____

Phone_____


Name_____

Address_____

_____

Phone_____

S

Name

Address

Phone

Name

Address

Phone

Name

Address

Phone

Name

Address

Phone

# S

Name

Address

Phone

Name

Address

Phone

Name

Address

Phone

Name

Address

Phone

T

Name

Address

Phone

Name

Address

Phone

Name

Address

Phone

Name

Address

Phone

T

Name

Address

Phone

Name

Address

Phone

Name

Address

Phone

Name

Address

Phone

# T

Name

Address

Phone

Name

Address

Phone

Name

Address

Phone

Name

Address

Phone

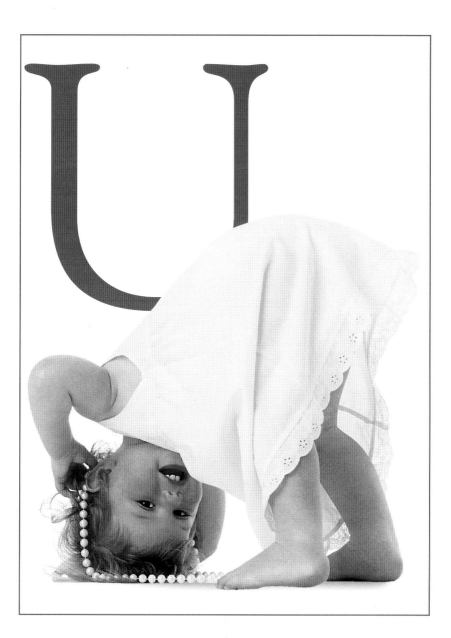

U

Name _____

Address _____

_____

Phone _____


Name _____

Address _____

_____

Phone _____


Name _____

Address _____

_____

Phone _____


Name _____

Address _____

_____

Phone _____

V

Name

Address

Phone

Name

Address

Phone

Name

Address

Phone

Name

Address

Phone

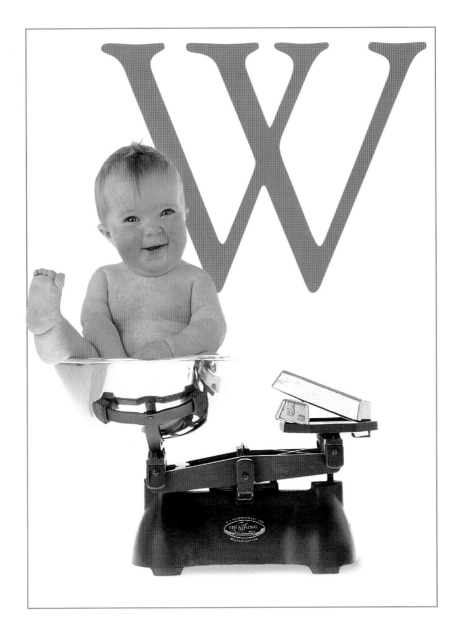

W

Name _____

Address _____

_____

Phone _____


Name _____

Address _____

_____

Phone _____


Name _____

Address _____

_____

Phone _____


Name _____

Address _____

_____

Phone _____

Name

Address

Phone

Name

Address

Phone

Name

Address

Phone

Name

Address

Phone

Name

Address

Phone

Name

Address

Phone

Name

Address

Phone

Name

Address

Phone

XYZ

Name

Address

Phone

Name

Address

Phone

Name

Address

Phone

Name

Address

Phone

X Y Z

Name

Address

Phone


Name

Address

Phone


Name

Address

Phone


Name

Address

Phone